The Lost Fragments of Heraclitus

The Lost Fragments *of* Heraclitus

Aphorisms

Neil Carpathios

RESOURCE *Publications* · Eugene, Oregon

THE LOST FRAGMENTS OF HERACLITUS
Aphorisms

Resource Publications
An Imprint of Wipf and Stock Publishers
199 W. 8th Ave., Suite 3
Eugene, OR 97401

www.wipfandstock.com

PAPERBACK ISBN: 978-1-6667-5490-2
HARDCOVER ISBN: 978-1-6667-5491-9
EBOOK ISBN: 978-1-6667-5492-6

VERSION NUMBER 122222

Introduction

So, how did it come to pass that I was able to discover the lost fragments of Heraclitus? How could such a monumental development in the world of philosophy and language occur without wide notice? Surely, multiple news outlets and academic journals would announce this startling discovery . . .

First, a bit about the man, Heraclitus.

Heraclitus was one of the early Pre-Socratic philosophers who sought to identify the origins for the creation of the world, and life's meaning. He lived in Ephesus (western Asia Minor, modern day Turkey) around 500 BC. His central claim is summed up in the phrase *Panta Rhei* ("life is flux"), recognizing the essential underlying essence of life as change. This, and various concepts concerning a single, eternal God who is behind all things and who set all in motion, which he called *Logos*. In Greek, *Logos* means "the word" but also means "to speak" and can also refer to "conveying thought." *Logos,* then, is a universal force or consciousness which created the universe and maintains it—as God would.

The ideas of Heraclitus are known to us strictly through the over 100 fragments which were discovered, attributed, and passed on by other Greek philosophers of the period. The original source, a large work written on papyrus, did not survive. Yet, in the history of this planet, these scant remaining fragments have influenced thinkers ever since, especially those in the Stoic school of thought. "Nothing is permanent except change." "One cannot step twice into the same river." And so on.

Heraclitus was known to his contemporaries as the "dark" philosopher, because his writings were so obscure and difficult to understand, composed in the form of riddle-like aphorisms. Scholars believe that they were written to force a reader toward independent thought and realization (much like the Zen koans of the Zen school of Buddhism). He was also referred to as "dark" because he was known to be sarcastic, critical, and prone to depression.

Scholars place his death at about 475 BC at the age of sixty. He is said to have died either by suicide or in a failed attempt to cure himself of a disease he was suffering from because he had no trust in doctors or anyone else. I suppose suicide could be considered an attempt—a permanent attempt—at a cure for mental and spiritual anguish. Based on what others wrote about him, no conclusive motive exists.

Now, back to the lost fragments . . .

I have always been fascinated with Heraclitus and his aphoristic micro-statements. Also, as a poet, I value brevity, compression, and evocation of thought and form. I am a big fan of the stylistic device known as aphorisms. Indeed, much of the poet's work involves finding ways to cram ideas or images into a tight space. Aphorisms may be the tightest of all spaces. But I digress . . .

In December of 2019, the COVID-19 pandemic was born. In March of that year, the university where I was teaching suddenly shut down, seemingly overnight.

Indeed, much of normal life came to a screeching halt. Masks, quarantines, shut-downs all became a new normal. Like many others, I suddenly found myself isolated from co-workers, and even family and friends. Like many others, throughout the subsequent months, I found myself moody, brooding, often depressed. I stopped writing poetry. I felt frozen inside, overwhelmed. I just didn't feel any inspiration. Instead I became a news-watching zombie. However, I did finally, gradually, start to take some creative baby steps. I gave myself permission to write down anything. I forced myself to stop pressuring my muse into churning out whole, polished poems. Even if I wrote a single line or two, that was enough. I remembered one of my heroes, Heraclitus, and his fragments. I started to fill up my notebooks with my own fragments. But were they really my own? I realized that I was sixty years old, the age the great philosopher died. Like him, I was seeking my own "cure" for my impotent state of mind. But thankfully, I was not quite suicidal . . .

Also, at this time of social isolation, as a diversion, a curiosity, I did something I always wanted to do. I took an ancestry test. I knew that both of my parents were from Greece. Both came from far eastern regions—my mother from the island of Rhodes which is closer to the mainland of Turkey than Greece, and my father from the island of Karpathos (thus, my name). So, I anticipated very Greek results. However, I was slightly surprised to find that my ancestry also showed evidence of roots in western Asia Minor. Although I have not ultimately found out, it is not outlandish that my roots could extend to the area of Ephesus (western Turkey), Heraclitus' home, which was an ancient Greek city at the time. Could I be in the bloodline of Heraclitus? It is possible. Perhaps my whole adult life writing short poetic forms, my obsession with understatement and linguistic compression, could be due to some ancient DNA wiring shared with the dark philosopher. Could this also be why I suddenly found myself writing my own fragments? At the age of sixty? In a world consumed by the specter of death like never before in my life? And at a moment when my creativity waned and my spirit was faltering?

I like to believe that in the year 2019, I began channeling the soul of Heraclitus. I like to believe that he, perhaps my great-great... uncle, reached out to me from the beyond in my time of stress. I like to believe that he helped guide the pen in my hand as I filled my notebooks with little phrases and thoughts, daily. As a man of faith in the invisible, I would never rule out such a possibility.

So, what follows, here, are the results of my pandemic scribblings. Unlike Heraclitus' famous fragments, some of these might be considered closer to the *gregueria*—a short form roughly similar to the traditional aphorism, but given to the surreal and to humor, made famous by its originator, Ramon Gomez de la Serna of Spain in the early 1900's. I like to believe that my uncle Heraclitus wanted to insert some lighter wit and flourishes to my thinking, at times, to counter the gloomy cloud of COVID-19. Overall, these fragments do strain toward enlightenment in a pursuit of spiritual embrace. But as co-author, he wanted me to have just a little bit of fun here and there. Maybe he learned to value a brighter vision after death. Maybe he was not the dismal, dark philosopher of legend. Thanks, Uncle Heraclitus!

The reader will, of course, see that these fragments lack much of the genius of Heraclitus' original jottings. Who could rival the great philosopher? However, I like to believe that his spirit didn't mind me falling short of perfection. His spirit wanted his nephew to do *most* of the writing even though his ghost hand also held the pen.

So, these are the lost fragments of Heraclitus (now found). The fragments, also, of Carpathios. To borrow from another of my literary heroes, Jorge Luis Borges, who wrote about his own psychic twin, his own co-author self: "I do not know which of us has written this page" ("Borges and I"). I do not know at this very second as I type these words if it is my fingers bouncing over the keys or those of my uncle Heraclitus—or both of us.

Finally, my uncle and I would like to thank David Lazar, editor of the fine magazine, *Hotel Amerika*, in which some of these fragments previously appeared. His devotion to the aphoristic is well documented.

Into every life a little brain must fall.

*

Nothing is ever truly gone, but just out of sight behind
the Great Sofa Cushion of the Universe.

*

Passion is indifference with a knife to its throat.

*

In the fall the leaves fall, and take their
leave, wiser than us.

*

We are happy to lose weight but distressed to lose hair. It
is the thing, not the act, that defines us.

*

To sleep, knowing that you are sleeping, is to be awake.

*

We say the water hugs the shore.
The sand kisses the water.
Underground, the roots of all the trees hold hands.
The wind whispers and sighs, and dies.

Is it loneliness or arrogance (or both)
how we decorate the world with more of us?

*

When all emotion is wringed out,

what is left is logic.

Then the rag is dry. Bone dry.
More tidy, less messy.
But stiff.

*

Penguins eat small fish.
Sea lions eat the penguins.
Great White Sharks eat the sea lions.
We eat the sharks and the sharks eat us.

*

To learn how the mirror works, look into it.

*

Gravity is the personal assistant of humiliation.

*

 Like dogs, we try scratching the itch we can't reach.

*

Hope is desperation on steroids.

*

Meditation is boredom with a purpose.

*

To die is to give birth to something called death.

*

Sweat is jealous of tears because eyes are drama queens.

*

We don't fall in love. We fall through it.

*

To be undead is to be born. To be unborn is to be dead.
In between is what you're reading and can't unread.

*

The only difference between *here* and *there* is a
"t" and a prayer.

*

The number of possibilities for our ultimate self decreas-
es with time. Unless we admit there is no ultimate self.

*

If we could know the dimensions of each other's loneli-
ness we would never be alone.

*

Every day I play dead so that death will not kill me.

*

We are all statues that think we are running.

*

Praying is the art of talking to yourself without a mask.

*

Children in a sandbox pretend it is a desert. People in a
church pretend to not pretend.

*

The missing hole in the middle is what makes the donut.
What makes God is what is missing.

*

This drama of life: We don't need props; we
need each other.

*

The empty theater teaches more than the packed house.

*

We try to make more and more money. Children fill
their pockets with dirt and stones.

*

Try not being longing's slave. Try flying like a bird.

*

Freedom is not the bird's flight, but its decision wheth-
er or not to fly.

*

Each time death comes, it scares me back to life.

*

Most men get married to manufacture new mothers.

*

Getting hurt or sick makes a doctor a better doctor.
Having a broken heart makes a lover a better lover.

*

The frozen pond does not know it is being skated across.
What skates across us?

*

Mountains and oceans exist to remind us
how small we are.

*

History: The remote control for our memory
needs new batteries.

*

Penguins give pebbles. Gorillas sniff each other's
armpits. We buy each other drinks and try to fall in
love, or try not to.

*

A happy marriage: To see each other with eyes deeply
knowing that one of you will die first and the other
one will suffer.

*

Because the burger isn't bloody in the middle doesn't
mean it wasn't once living.

*

Look at all the toys whose batteries have run out. Look at
all the graves.

*

All grapes droop toward the ripeness they were born for.

*

The tree that is tired of being a tree is still
trapped in bark.

*

A mosquito drinks blood through a straw on its body.
Who knows what God is or how thirsty?

*

The stop sign never sleeps.

*

We rely on things we know are unreliable. It
feels good to rely.

*

There is no detox for selfishness.

*

The crows do not know that in a group they are
called a murder.
When we are together, what do we not know?

*

In debt is not the same as poor.

*

On the presence of God: The wind has no color, but we know it is there.

*

Every color waves goodbye to its white. When we're born, what do we wave goodbye to?

*

The invisible expiration date on our forehead: branded like cattle in the womb.

*

When in doubt, ask the sunlight—it is weightless and free.

*

Wear yourself inside-out to color-coordinate with everyone.

*

A water glass can't contain the whole ocean. A brain can't possess all mystery.
We are small, small vessels.

*

Believe nothing but what you can see, and you're blind.

*

We are the only animal that displays a big stone to tell the world we passed through.

*

Where does the dark go when we turn on a lamp?

*

Smoke tries to retain its vagueness. Like fog. Clarity isn't everything.

*

Between us is a secret held between parentheses.

*

At least once a day I lie down on the magic carpet of someone's voice.

*

Your very pores make you holy.

*

A wince is a smile's jealous cousin.

*

Did the table, the chair ever thank its tree?

*

Fingerprints are eternity's ripples the dropped stone of each breath makes on the surface of your life.

*

A hug is a whole body kiss. Death is when life hugs us too hard.

*

When we're young we hatch into adults. When we're old
we spend our days trying to glue back together the pieces
of the shell we broke through.

*

Study the ant that can't lift and carry off the fallen
potato chip. How he takes a small nibble—what he can
do—then moves on.

*

Rip off the band-aid, but sip the wine slowly.

*

When picking up a broken toy, be careful not to
stir its hopes.

*

Happiness is a small shrub in our front yard we walk past
every day without seeing.

*

A worm cut in half goes on living. What is self-pity?

*

One leaf accepts its fate. Another, next to it on the
branch, clings.

*

Pebbles know that their cousins are mountains.

9

*

In the language of doors, hello and goodbye
are the same word.

*

A scarecrow is a Christ crucified in corn.

*

An olive in a martini is one lucky olive.

*

There once was an ice cube that melted itself then froze
itself then melted itself then froze itself, alternating back
and forth day after day to defy physics and prove death
can be conquered, and that inside of every ice cube are
hidden countless lives. All the other ice cubes followed
suit starting the Revolt of the Ice Cubes. Then I woke up.

*

A knife slurps when you cut a melon. When you cut
your finger it licks itself.

*

Does the wind need the wind chime, or does the wind
chime need the wind?

*

Today is just like yesterday, but in different clothes.

*

The Buddhists are right: All suffering comes from attachment. But most happiness too.

*

The floor and the ceiling are like birth and death. In between the two is where living goes on.

*

A blade of grass never heard of a birthday or a funeral.

*

We all want something: money, toys, lovers, wisdom, happiness. Wanting less—less stress, less clutter, less distraction— is still wanting.

*

Every ice cream flavor thinks it is the best.

*

Thank God for this. Thank heavens for that. Even language prays.

*

The sound of a distant train reminds us our bodies are anchors. The white trail of a jet overhead, too.

*

Because God couldn't be everywhere at once, he invented mothers.

*

Sometimes a shadow goes looking for its person.

*

That eyes can't see them, during the day, doesn't mean
the stars shine less.

*

You don't think the mind plays tricks? Why does wine
taste different in a wine glass than in a jar?

*

The man who wastes time constructively is my hero.

*

Everywhere we look is *before* and *after* photos. Is as
is ever possible?

*

The quieter the path, the louder your footsteps.

*

Whoever hears the sound of one hand clap-
ping is psychotic.

*

A stone dropped in water sinks to the bottom. A feather
floats on top. No thing can deny its nature.

*

The crack in the rock is not the rock's fault.

*

Just because we can't hear the screams, a worm on a
hook still damns us for eternity.

*

We think we own our life, but it is a small rental—which
is more than enough.

*

Something opening is something closing in reverse.

*

Sometimes a desperate clock that wants us to
love it, stops.

*

I am the mirror's ghost writer. We are working on his
memoir titled, *Face to Face*.

*

Under the eyelid the eye sees plenty.

*

An ant doesn't care how old he is.

*

They say that our shoulder blades are where we'll have
wings. We are desperate to be more than this meat.

*

When we're alone we're with everyone we've ever known. Which gets crowded. Which is why we get in the car and go to a bar or store or coffee shop—to be around people.

*

A wave is most itself becoming another wave.

*

The devil: Sometimes he gets tired of orchestrating disasters and early deaths, takes the day off—which is when it is highly recommended to sit outside as the sun goes down, a chilled glass of white wine, some pistachios in a bowl, with or without a companion, as the crickets start their pick-up lines which sounds like music, nothing hurried or wasted, because you can bet your sweet life tomorrow that bastard will be rested, refreshed, raring to get up and go back to business.

*

Oh sweat bee mining the deep wrinkle in my neck, enjoy yourself before my hand like a giant hammer thrown down from heaven nails you into blood on my palm at about the spot where a nail was pounded through Christ's flesh.

*

Christ's hand nailed to a tree. Because this moment it's what I see. Even if it is just a glove.

*

I wake up and the mile-high neon-lit exit sign is bigger and clearer than yesterday. And in the mirror, the crumpled candy wrapper of my face. How did this happen?

*

If our bodies are women who are never meant to be faithful to us, I suspect mine is secretly seeing someone else. She keeps making excuses when I invite her to go to the gym or even jog in the neighborhood the way we used to do. *Too tired* is her favorite.

*

Blinking is for chopping up the day into ten thousand individual pieces.

*

I know why daisies avoid us. All those *she loves me, she loves me nots*. They stand, stuck, anchored in dirt, helpless. When we walk by, they hold their breath, try to be invisible.

*

One snowman told me he never asked to be born. He described how cold it gets overnight under stars. And contrary to popular belief, that it feels good to melt.

*

When they opened him, they found his body was a
Russian Nesting Doll containing infinite replicas, each
enclosing a smaller one, each hollow except for the
last, his innermost self that prior to this existed only in
theory. No wonder in life he felt so heavy. No wonder the
recurring dream that he was an egg. How he could feel
them pushing, all his future selves impatient, growing.
No wonder the older he got, all those cracks on his skin.

*

The sound of small rocks and dirt hitting the wood of the
coffin. Beyond sadness or hope. Earth gets dug. Some-
thing's planted. Does something bloom?

*

I filled my house with my worries, until I ran out of
room. Then I built a shed I filled up too. I paid for self-
storage. Being a parent requires lots of space.

*

On my to-do list:

1. construct a bell that when struck emits silence

2. witness a blizzard in August

3. just for fun, talk ocean waves into going on strike,
   refusing to roll, flat as glass

*

Snowflake: Are you God's frozen teardrop? Are the Buddhists right, that you never fall in the wrong place? Are your six crystal arms desperately reaching for other flakes? Was my grade school teacher correct that no two of you are alike, despite recent studies that assert at the molecular level you are all the same? Is your hexagonal beauty due to anything other than chance? Are you like I was the instant I landed, sensing the visit here would be brief?

*

Crazy ant trying to hoist the fallen pretzel all by yourself. Call your buddies. You have my word. I'll keep an eye out for the neighbor's pooch always unleashed and scrounging.

*

Deadline. The word must hate itself for containing death. Can't fathom the simple concept of a date to complete a task. All it knows is the end of something. Who wants *dead* in their name? Does it ever try to end itself?

*

Junk mail: I don't need a hernia mesh, whatever that is. Or cream to extend my erections (well, maybe just a little). Or a Russian bride, or a Walmart voucher. Or a new device that speeds up my metabolism. Or the chance to win a million dollars. World, keep sending your options. You seem to think you know what's best. But that's in the other room. A sweet wicked angel, my soulmate. Running a brush through her long blond hair.

*

I am a former baby, a future skeleton, a distant future pile of dust.

*

When we pray, we press our two palms together as if they are kissing.

*

The perfect cure for any sadness: the cosmic pep talk of a child's eyes.

*

The man on the science show claims it all comes down to particles, quarks, and atomic nuclei. Not some childish addiction to metaphor. Everything can and will be explained, he says. Then explain how when my wife touches me her hands become butterflies. And will I be able to smoke cigars and drink wine in the afterlife, or at least swing on a tree swing, naked in the dark? Is there anything not attached by its invisible cord to everything else? Was that my dead mother just now when the chalk squeaked on the blackboard, playing tricks with her new voice?

*

Tiniest nail in the house of the universe, you do your job well.

*

Confession: When the landlord keeps my deposit, citing a dime-sized stain on the carpet, I get out my voodoo doll kit.

*

Men mowing lawns. Every other day they push mow-
ers. The grass has grown microscopically since the day
before. I admire their diligence, and their precise rows.
From my porch I watch them, these fellow-mortals.
I am taking notes for our species. We call each other
neighbor. From Old English, meaning *near inhabitant*.
Good men with beer guts and a strange obsession with
short grass. I've noticed, they do not like shoveling snow
nearly as much.

*

Pulling weeds I discover a toad. Its reptilian stare is
indecipherable. If it were a thousand times bigger,
dinosaur-ish, men in tanks would flee. But it is a golf-ball
with eyes, leathery, squat, scaly-covered, endearing as a
cartoon character. Not the most charismatic or sexy of
beings, like, say, a leopard or wild stallion. But the google
eyes hold all the things it has learned from being alive
inside that bumpy skin. All you can ask of any creature.

*

I wear this human shape so as not to terrify wife,
children, friends. Sometimes I think the neighbor's
cat knows what I really am, the way she stares at me
from their stoop.

*

To the dragonfly, an airplane is God.

*

I told the last banana it was more beautiful with bruises.
My one daily good deed.

*

The crow is ordinary, common. But look how it
perches on the lip of a trash bin, staring down into all
our human muck.

*

The woman peeing under the bridge lifts her skirt and
squats, oblivious to cars on each side racing past. Dog-
like, she's done what she needed to do, and in any god's
eyes I'm sure she's loved no less.

*

The cardboard sign the homeless man holds on the street
corner is not homemade since he has no home.

*

Ask a leaf how it accepts its fate.
Ask the spider whose web you tatter, already rebuilding,
how it doesn't give up.
Ask a butterfly how to grow wings.
Ask flies orbiting shit the secret of happiness.

*

Are politicians kissing babies really God sticking His
finger down His own throat to vomit?

*

Today I caught my mirror dreaming of faces.

*

The matches sleeping in the matchbox: their tiny blue
heads dream of small explosions.
Look how shirts on a clothesline puff out their chests.
How a desperate hat flees down a sidewalk, a fat lady
wobbling after it.
How a pencil in a mug remembers once being sharp.
How moon dust through the window spells
names on the floor.

*

An ant crosses the kitchen's linoleum with what ap-
pears to be a tiny suitcase and one-way ticket. Is the
potted plant on the window sill thinking how lucky, or
how melodramatic?

*

How far back, memory? A slab of meat on a conveyer
belt receiving a soul?

*

For every suicide there are at least one hundred births.
For every tumor, some kisses.

*

The wasted day begs to be invited back.

*

To be alive, squared. To live vividly. To let your eyes be
windows and watch moments drift by like clouds.

*

Sunlight lures out of every object a smaller version of
itself in a black suit.

*

My younger days were frantic running. Now I traipse
like a butterfly on a piece of cheese.

*

Everyone, at least once, should experience guzzling
cheap whiskey under a single light bulb dangling from a
wire in the kitchen at midnight, alone, on Christmas Eve.

*

The rain is sweetest to the parched grass.

*

If you like dancing, don't be afraid to sweat.

*

No cloud fears disappearing.

*

Children on a playground don't ask what time it is.

*

A drowning man is never tall enough.

*

You want sadness? I thought so…An old woman kneels
beside a grave whispering something before she leans in
to kiss the chiseled name on the stone. A little girl, as she
studies herself in a mirror, wonders if it's possible to scis-
sor off fat rolls from around her waist.

*

Ars Poetica: A dog barks to keep himself com-
pany. Pretends the barking echo is some other dog
calling out to him.

*

The squash growing bulbous-warty are not jealous of
the sexy red tomatoes or the intoxicating basil. But
sometimes, even they, in their dreams, run away to Hol-
lywood and become pineapples.

*

The little boy riding an invisible pony has never heard of
a mortgage or acid reflux. His only concern is to hold on
and stay in his stirrups, as they leap and float past a little
girl waltzing with an invisible prince.

*

My children's old toys crammed into a box taped shut,
stored in the attic. They sniff cardboard walls, prisoners
of the dark. They tolerate tiny footsteps of spiders. Spend
their days and nights praying for small hands to reach in
and lift them into the light.

*

After weeks of no rain, the trees—if you listen closely—
are whistling for dogs.

*

You said, "My thoughts are with you." They
must be invisible.

*

This disguise of flesh. Human costume. So as not to spill
out our souls, like moonlight or water.

*

Silence always gets the last word.

*

A successful failure. At least I achieved that.

*

A dress with a woman not in it.
A shirt on a hanger.
Is this how the dead see themselves crossing over?

*

Every day I give the mirror my face. And he gives it back.

*

To make a bed a living bed, you have to make love in it.
Until then, the bed is dead.

*

The sky is pregnant. We are children of the wind.

*

Cats sniff each other's asses. We watch reality TV.

*

Comprehend existence? Try to cram the sky into a jar.

*

If there is a God, He has no ears, no answering machine—and still we call.

*

Being born is walking into a room, looking back over your shoulder, and the door has disappeared. Dying is when, one day, the door suddenly appears again.

*

We are all half-way out on a rope bridge that's fraying.

*

Today I applauded a tomato, made it blush even redder.

*

If Jesus were here, would he ask me for a dollar?

*

We are like doors that once were trees.

*

The heart is a grenade.

*

If I could only drag the sea behind me like a
child with a puppy.

*

I wish I spoke moon, or wind, or grass, or ocean. Maybe
I do. Could they be shy or pretending not to hear?

*

Locks hide keys from us to show who's boss.

*

Living with Scars is our collective memoir.

*

We treat dogs like people, and each other like dogs.

*

The creaky floor wants our footsteps to remember.

*

I threw the anchor unattached to a rope. Stupid or brave?

*

Raindrops are the sky's pebbles.

*

There cannot be just one of *us*.

*

Today's gem: A girl kicks her butt with her own heels as she runs. Then she stops and combs sunlight from her doll's hair.

*

Leaves rustling. What is it the wind is searching for in the trees?

*

Your face is never the face another face sees.

*

I borrow from time to pay it back later.

*

We can all afford to pay attention.

*

My thoughts without me are everyone's thoughts.

*

Perfect discipline is most admired by those who fear spontaneity.

*

The classical musician studies notes. The jazz musician creates them.

*

Adult love: To walk in two different directions but remain side by side.

*

To possess a thing is to be possessed.

*

The ripest fruit is the messiest.

*

Whatever is trapped inside of a raindrop may as well
enjoy the view.

*

Whoever claims he has all the answers still wears diapers.

*

Last night's dream: I saw Christ's shadow on dirt just
before his last breath.

*

Tell a tree not to grow. Tell a stone to sprout wings. The
world is the world.

*

Change. Stay the same. Your death doesn't care.

*

Sunlight refuses to let the world give up.

*

It takes the darkness to make us all look alike.

*

We were made the perfect size for holding
joy. And sadness.

*

A brief encounter with your true self is a blind date with
the Devil. And God.

*

It is more like it is now than it ever was before.

*

Time and wounds live for each other.

*

The right path is never a path.

*

Locked doors expect to be knocked on.

*

The best disguise is no disguise.

*

Technology helps us forget our fangs and claws.

*

An ape in a fancy suit is still an ape.

*

Poetry recycles loneliness into something more valuable
we mostly ignore.

29

*

Being free is accepting being unfree.

*

At the end of my life I hope I'll be able to say
thank you to myself.
The music of time: past, present, future—
all the same note.

*

If stars had hands they'd sew our mouths shut.

*

Moonlight tries to make the roadkill beautiful for us.

*

Walking on the beach at sunrise I give up my opinions.

*

When a tree dies the forest says a prayer.

*

Holy places soaked with blood.
Priests who molest little boys.
God must shake His head and ask for a double.

*

A man with ambition needs a little death to yank the
carpet from under him.

*

Sometimes a dog eats with its nose.

*

She owns a perfect butt, and her butt owns me.

*

There are treasures already in our pockets. I swear
the moon said so.

*

After chopping wood on a tree stump for two hours, I
like the world again.

*

To truly taste the wine requires somebody
to drink it with.

*

A grape doesn't resist becoming a raisin.

*

How lucky in one life to watch fireflies remind us
why we're here.

*

When I look up at the stars I think of the fish that
told another fish how he'd heard stories that there is
another world above the water's surface out there. To
which his buddy replied, "You must be crazy, this is
the only world."

*

Bees see our faces as strange flowers.
We see our faces as just faces.
Bees orbit close, in love with us.
We turn away from each other's face.

*

Stars leak light for us to drink until we're happy, drunk.

*

The puddle reflects the streetlight at night
without an agenda.

*

No book can read itself. Who I am I'll never know.

*

The music in the piano doesn't exist without the pianist.

*

Every face is a mirror.

*

Like a microchip inserted in us in the womb, loneliness
exists to help us appreciate each other more.

*

The one thing we all share no matter who or where we
are: this very second.

*

Learning to be alone takes more energy than pushing through a maddening crowd.

*

Today is the perfect day because I want it to be.

*

The old starlit had her face redone. Like a fallen leaf trying to reattach itself to the branch.

*

To be as tough as a nail you must be a nail.

*

A note on my windshield pointing out that I parked too close. The smiley face and the *fuck you* were unnecessary.

*

On an elevator we stare at our shoes. Or up at the numbers changing. Avoiding each other's eyes as if they'll see into us.

*

I could hear everyone's thoughts in the room before they became words. When the speaking began the thoughts changed.

*

Turn down the lights to hear the music better.

*

The way bubble wrap protects something fragile, dis-
tracting ourselves cushions us.

*

Sometimes an open door is the hardest one
to walk through.

*

At my age, even in a traffic jam, why would I want time
to move faster?

*

Sometimes you're so lonely even the telemarketer's voice
on the phone is a friend.

*

Once, I considered ending it all, when through the win-
dow I saw my son's tricycle.

*

We touch each other to remind ourselves we
are still here.

*

Like cicadas that wait for years to explode through the
ground, our lives are a preparation to launch.

*

Silence teaches us how to listen.

*

For most of us, words are clothes off the rack. For poets, words must be tailor-made.

*

When I say *I love you*, the words can't come close to what I really mean. But a crumb is better than starving.

*

That jet plane overhead—I am on it, looking out the window at myself far below looking up.

*

I am still learning how to be in more than one place at once. Every day the wind says I'm not ready to be wind.

*

The Greek sculptures look like Olympic athletes. Did they all work out at the same gym?

*

Somewhere inside the stem, does the rose know that its petals will fall?

*

Who sprinkled these flaws all over me I spend my life trying to scrub off?

*

Somewhere, this very second, is the beginning of a story that ends somewhere this very second.

*

In whose mind as a memory do I dance?

*

Not every grape can become wine.

*

At dusk, the day asked me to sit down and join it.

*

All things in moderation, the Greeks said. But sometimes I want to party with the gypsies!

*

Every raindrop explodes on impact. Every person says goodbye.

*

We decorate our prison cell to feel more in charge.

*

The soundless ballroom of the body: what's inside each one of us.

*

A late Friday afternoon meeting, when all I want is a martini and her naked breasts. They say everything has its exact inverse somewhere in the universe. Is it even possible that out there somewhere someone thinks: A martini and her naked breasts, when all I want is a late Friday afternoon meeting?

*

The taste of the pear is temporary. The memory of the taste of the pear lingers on. When even memory is gone, where does the taste go?

*

Forever is man-made. Like a small sculpture we keep on a shelf. Model of something more perfect than what we have, which for some reason is never enough.

*

I don't need *forever*. But sometimes I need the small crescent scar on her ankle she says only I know is there.

*

In a dream God said: "I'll show you THE perfect sunset, if you show me exactly what it feels like to be you."

*

Today while I ate the orange I imagined I would die at the end of the day. Some orange!

*

Every day I should be a slightly better me. Even if no one sees it.

*

Some vegetarians like to pretend they can't hear the whispered conversations of carrots.

*

I like a little tongue with my kiss. I like to sweat when I dance. I like my meat a little bloody in the middle.

*

Rowing across a lake with a peanut butter sandwich and thermos of coffee as the sun comes up. Thank you.

*

Was I born to witness the single sweat bead rolling down the small of her back like a diamond in this candle-lit room?

*

To fill a basket you must empty it first.

*

I can look all I want and not see.

*

Vividness plus compression plus music equals poetry.

*

The best teacher learns from the worst student.

*

If my life were a sentence, even if I wanted an exclamation, it would end with a question mark.

*

If you want the ripest tomato, pick it yourself.

*

An aphorism is what we already know minus the fluff,
which makes it look new.

*

To lure a truth to the surface like a fish requires patience,
silence, a little luck, and secret bait that only you can
put on the hook.

*

Because we like closure, we call it *catch*,
not playing *throw*.

*

We open the bottle and let the wine breathe, and the
wine thanks us by sacrificing itself.

*

We say the clock has a face, the chair a back, the table
four legs. We say books have spines, the shoe a tongue,
the wine bottle a long slender neck. The watch has hands.
The lettuce is a head. Even the cigarette has a butt. Here
we go again: Why do we humanize all things not us?

*

All things die. Even pens run out of ink.

*

My ears tell my brain what the sound is. Sometimes my
brain tells my ears to stop showing off.

*

Seek and ye shall find—and if you don't, at least you'll find nothing.

*

Improvement isn't always fun. Sometimes you have to pluck a stray hair even if it hurts.

*

To become a great scar requires a deep wound.

*

Even the atheist thanks God it's Friday.

*

Lust is a lit fuse.

*

When we walk into a crowded room, we watch ourselves being watched.

*

Some have a knack for annoying; others have a knack for being annoyed. Two puzzle pieces made for each other.

*

Stupid is wrong squared.

*

He can't help being the way he is, but does he have to
be it around me?

*

It takes a puddle, or dog doo-doo, to make you
watch your step.

*

The best lesson for a reckless bird is a closed window.

*

Getting somewhere requires leaving the house.

*

A comma never hurries.

*

Patience is a virtue unless inaction is a crime.

*

I'm dying for that piece of cake. But really, I'm just dying.
I live for you. But really, I'm just living.

*

I could live without you. The way a bird with amputated
wings, earth-bound, wobbles.

*

The decision was a no-brainer. Me loving you
is a no-hearter.

＊

As the scalpel is to the surgeon, and the saw is to the carpenter, and imagination is to the poet, compassion should be to all of us.

＊

Something doesn't have to be real to exist.

＊

There are ambitions for a larger cause, and there are ambitions for the self. Neither is wrong, but the former is worth more effort.

＊

You cannot change who you are, but you can change what you are.

＊

The soul eats what the mind cooks.

＊

It takes winter to truly feel spring.

＊

The moth seems mad to enter the lightbulb, battering it-self over and over. Which brings to mind religious fervor.

＊

One intimate kiss is worth ten thousand handshakes.

＊

Life after life starts with death.

                    *

The way the wet leaf on the sidewalk leaves a stain, we
imprint each other.

                    *

Target my wounds with your kisses.
Heal me.

                    *

A true traveler carries the road, within.

                    *

There is so much to say about *Nothing*. Which is why we
have poets. Which is why all poems fail.

                    *

Language tries to fit experience, like a fat man squeezing
into children's clothes.

                    *

If there is a God, He must be taking a nap.

                    *

If I hold your hand, you must hold mine.

                    *

Only the circle knows where it begins and ends.

                    *

You can't build a house without hammering the
nails in straight.

*

The child knows that inside the shell, the peanut sleeps.

*

Some days I'm stale bread. Some days I'm moldy cheese.
But at least I'm something, which is better than nothing.

*

Fish don't swim backwards.

*

"Oh well" equals "I don't care."

*

The future sneaks up on us; the past hides.

*

Even a genius stubs his toe.

*

Every metaphor moons us and grins.

*

Conformity is a dance hall with no dancers.

*

Sometimes eyes hear and ears see. And a nose knows.

*

Time flies, but where does it land?

*

The deaf hear God's voice; the blind see His face.

*

Sometimes in the prison yard the snow falls, and like children the prisoners watch.

*

God's favorite prank: a broken condom.

*

The aphorism that strains to be profound, kills itself.

*

If everybody always bowled a perfect game, who would want to bowl?

*

Dream big. Work bigger.

*

I'm not overwhelmed or underwhelmed. Just whelmed.

*

That we live and die is obvious. The rest is pretty damn confusing.

*

When I watch and hear politicians, all I can think of is dirty diapers.

*

When we choose a mate, we really are saying *reveal me to myself.*

*

The sky coughs clouds and spits rain.

*

When asked if she wanted more, the Buddhist answered "less, please."

*

How many bad haircuts until I realize the problem is my face?

*

Frozen peas sound like glass tears hitting the plate.

*

In the frying pan, the egg grew an eye in death.

*

Can past life hypnosis reveal to the bacon its pig?

*

Evangelists are most frightening always.

*

The connoisseur of sunsets self-medicates by looking.

*

Both pleasure and pain remind us we're slaves.

*

Boring sermons taught me how to sleep with my eyes
open. A technique I still use at dull parties and meetings.

*

Sex without love is like a pizza with no cheese.

*

Failure is a strict teacher that doesn't bend the rules.

*

Even a lobster in a boiling pot can't soften a heart.

*

In the presence of a vacuum, does a broom
feel inadequate?

*

Do windows attempt suicide by luring reckless birds, and
do birds attempt suicide like little kamikazes?

*

Do some trash cans believe the garbage is their fault?

*

The Zen master plays musical chairs with no
chairs and no music.

*

On a crowded, cramped bus nostrils wish they weren't.

*

Our flaws unite us.

*

Life is not a game, yet we continue to toy with each other.

*

Snow angels are craters left where real angels land after
jumping off of clouds to kill themselves.

*

Somewhere between constipation and diarrhea lies the
secret of happiness.

*

A bite can't bite itself.

*

Improvisation is routine letting its hair down.

*

A bridge exists to help others cross.

*

To notice the flowers along the way, take small steps.

*

The narcotic of money is addictive. Why isn't there a
Moneyaholics Anonymous?

*

Something must be done about all these drunk telephone
poles swerving into the street.

*

All the fake smiles that have ever been photographed
prove we're trained monkeys.

*

The puppet that knows it's a puppet broods.

*

Now, nower, nowest—are all the same. Or are they?

*

A bird watches a man fall off a high cliff, and grins.

*

Solitude is loneliness understood.

*

Mannequin as a verb: to *mannequin* is to ignore.
Don't mannequin me.

*

All the great thinkers throughout time are our tour
guides, but sometimes we have to wander through
the streets alone.

*

A novel is a life, a short story is a day, a poem is an hour,
an aphorism is a blink.

*

To know the silence inside an ice cube,
you must be water.

*

Before a hole is born, where does it wait? My pock-
et wants to know.

*

A bear trap cannot catch a fly. A fly swatter can-
not stop a bear.

*

Comma: a sideways smile, a small fish-hook, a slow-
motion teardrop, a period that leaks.

*

The dark: It likes how I bump into furniture and curse. It
hopes I'll stub my toe. His favorite game is hide and seek
when I flick on the lamp.

*

We need help getting dressed for our funeral.

*

My first request after dying: the sound of every tree that ever fell in a forest when nobody was there.

*

My blisters, callouses, moles compete for my attention.

*

Invest in the future, but be present.

*

An armpit never sniffs itself.

*

We say birds sing, but they could be cursing each other. When we curse each other do birds think we sing?

*

The Hopper painting, *Nighthawks at the Diner*. Today's equivalent: Starbucks and every person texting or staring at a laptop.

*

Children stretch each other into adults.

*

Even without a leash, my pet loneliness tags along.

*

When I said her face was a can opener, she didn't
understand. I meant it's so pretty it can pry open
any man's heart.

*

My tongue is a red carpet in my mouth I roll out for you.

*

An erection is a kid in a classroom who doesn't know the
answer but sticks his hand up anyway.

*

Under the curse of the present moment, let's
find each other.

*

I signed a contract in the womb. I couldn't read the fine
print. Does it matter?

*

What allows us to live within the present moment most
authentically? This is the single question of existence that
weighs most heavily.

*

The best teacher of stoicism? A stone. It would do any-
thing to do nothing a little while longer.

*

I challenge the willfulness of objects, not when I break
them, but when I love them.

*

Time is God's big eraser every second erasing us.

*

The terminally insecure can't hide inside their clothes.

*

Only the aphorism embarrassed by its human source
is worth reading.

*

I ask my aphorisms how I'm doing. They don't reply. Do
they take an oath of silence? I can tell they want me to
close my notebook.

*

The aphorist gives birth to little pebbles of thought.
Or, more accurately, passes them—unlike the novel-
ist who suffers years of constipation trying to squeeze
out a mountain.

*

We all have to crack a little now and then, but we don't
have to shatter.

*

Is loving an art or a vocation?

*

Are we born perfect, a clean slate? Is the blank page the
most perfect in the book?

*

Our skeletons wear us until we wear out. Our skeletons speak to each other through our flesh.

*

I x-ray myself over and over hoping to spot something worth keeping.

*

Making a child and killing someone. Planting a seed, yanking a weed?

*

I have a double whose sole job is to catalogue and store my regrets, while I appear to everyone composed and content, free to skip and whistle a tune.

*

My double asks if we can trade places for just one day. I always tell him yes, for sure. Tomorrow.

*

The mask we show others is our personality. When we're alone and we take the mask off, we're left with our character.

*

I could see her eyes were exit wounds. What goes on inside her?

*

When we're young we rely on our looks. When we're old they rely on us.

*

A bathtub without a body in it. Nothing more despondent. How to know if the tub has committed suicide? If it doesn't turn warm when filled with hot water, you know it's too late.

*

Is all the sadness everywhere God playing dead so we'll give Him mouth-to-mouth? Is all that He wants, a kiss?

*

We occupy space like a lover then leave it.

*

Do roses dream of jumping down their stems?

*

I sense a reverse déjà vu: not that I've been here before but will never be again.

*

Through the door between women's legs, God sends reinforcements. In purple, screaming, pudgy packages He hides a drop of Himself. We die to make room for more of Him.

*

Snowflakes are angels' false eyelashes.

*

When people die they're not dead but just looking at us
through a two-way mirror.

*

Does the newspaper resent being tattooed with
all those deaths?

*

After a sleepless night, all day my pillow keeps sending
me messages to come home and kiss it.

*

The curiosity to know about your lover's former
lovers is like the itch of a chicken pox. If you
scratch it—good luck.

*

We need a little pain now and then, the way a can-
vas needs paint.

*

The first line of every religion's sacred text, if it's honest,
should read: *No one has the first clue why we're here.*

*

The only way to kill all fear is to kill the ego. Like smash-
ing a vessel so it can no longer hold polluted water.

*

The thermometer that measures my content-
ment is silence.

*

The tree wears a gown of snowflakes.

*

When I asked the boy what he was doing, he said gather-
ing up raindrops to return them to the clouds.

*

Our nipples are shy, until they meet.

*

To see what each other sees, we'd need to trade eyes. But
that would blind us.

*

That worm impersonating a comma needs to curl more.

*

This second, all over, worms crawl through eye sockets
and party in a skull.

*

A dead person lives in a grave.

*

When we die, do we graduate, or are we expelled?

*

The dog on a leash attached to the tree wants to walk it.

*

Do toll booth workers dream of being bank
tellers one day?

*

When I offer my desire a drink, it always asks for more.

*

I'd rearrange the stars for her. Does God think that
when He's in love?

*

What did he pack in the bags under his eyes the
way they bulge?

*

Just now a drunk in the alley screaming that his mother
never loved him. Or was that the wind?

*

Loneliness is a privilege, loneliness whispers, trying to
get us to love it.

*

The stubbed toe is a catastrophe to the foot.

*

When the braindrops fall, there is no
umbrella big enough.

Printed in Great Britain
by Amazon